TWENTY-SEVEN GROUPS OF EXERCISES

for

CORNET and TRUMPET

Designed to develop

Breath Control, Lip Flexibility, and the Muscular Embouchure

with Special Exercises in Triple and Double Tonguing

REVISED EDITION

by

EARL D. IRONS

Director of Bands
Arlington State College
Arlington, Texas

★

Text Edited by

C. M. O'NEAL, B.A., M.A., PH.D.

Prof. of English
Arlington State College

FOREWORD

Probably every musician who writes an instruction book for his instrument feels that he is somewhat presumptuous in doing so, since there are already so many fine methods written. Especially is this true of the writer of a book for cornet or trumpet. However, the ambitious student should have a complete library and should welcome new books that deal with a special phase of instrumental study. With this in view I feel that I have something valuable to offer, something in the nature of a specialized text. The exercises in this book have been written for the sole purpose of developing a smooth and almost effortless tone in both the high and low registers of the cornet and trumpet, and yet a tone based on a principle which allows the maximum of flexibility and ease in the execution of fast passages.

After studying and conversing with the very finest cornet players in this country I have worked out and compiled a series of exercises which have proved so beneficial to me that I feel they should be passed on to other teachers and players of the cornet and trumpet. These exercises are the result of much experimentation. First I tried the lip shift system, and found it effective for the actual production of high tones. After a while I could play, with very little effort and by blowing harder, tones up to second G above the staff *fortissimo*. However, I found that I could not execute fast passages and use the lip shift, and so concluded that this system was impractical for me. Similarly I tried other systems, but for me none seemed to be entirely satisfactory.

At last I began building an embouchure based on the scientific principles treated in this book. I tried all kinds of exercises. By elimination, combination, and constant testing I eventually found those which most effectively produced the desired results. I have demonstrated these exercises at numerous clinics, festivals, and contests. The series of exercises has met with such approval that I am putting it in book form.

I am not offering this work as a self-teaching method, but as an aid for the teacher, to be used in conjunction with any of the standard methods. At the same time I have designed the text to serve as a self help device for advanced players of cornet and trumpet who are not entirely satisfied with their range. I do not claim that this is the only method for perfecting the high register on cornet and trumpet, but I do claim that it is practical and effective.

The nine pages added to this book that have already been used by thousands of teachers and students of the cornet and trumpet will be of great aid in perfecting the triple and double tonguing. This different approach to the above mentioned type of tonguing will be revolutionary if practiced consistently. St. Jacone was the first, to my knowledge, to suggest this kind of tonguing. Ed Chenette brought it to my attention in 1949. Since that time I have been working on it and have changed my students from the old type of tonguing to the kind in the following exercises with great success.

These exercises should be practiced until the KU or K attack is just as positive and pleasing as the TU or T attack. This ease can only be attained by consistent practice. Each exercise should be played very, very slowly, with speed increasing gradually.

You will notice that the triple tonguing is nothing more than double tonguing divided into triplets. After this type of tonguing is perfected, it should make no difference whether the attack is on the T or K. At the very beginning it will be necessary for the student to use more diaphragm on the K than on the T attack. After a few weeks practice this will not be noticeable.

Pages 24 and 25 should be practiced very slowly with some space between each tone. Use the attack as marked. It may take only a few days for some, especially the young player, while it may take weeks of hard work for the student that has formed a habit of playing the old style system. In either case the student will be amply repaid for his efforts.

Speed can be gained in the following pages according to the ability of the student. Please keep this one thing in mind: speed will be of no worry if these exercises are properly worked out and consistently practiced. Pages 30 and 31 are taken from the Arban method as far as notes are concerned. Play each exercise many times, using both attacks as marked. Practice 45 to 45D with caution. Do not play higher than the embouchure will stand. Do not use excessive pressure.

The exercises on this last page are to be single tongued and will be found very beneficial in gaining power and endurance. The last nine pages of this book were written and compiled with the sincere hope that the exercises will help to eliminate some of the faulty triple and double tonguing that is so noticeable among most school age players. The Arban method has an abundance of material to further your studies in this type of tonguing — from page 155 to 190 inclusive.

With this brief foreword I submit to you twenty-seven groups of exercises for developing breath control, lip flexibility, and the muscular embouchure. I hope that you will find them as helpful to you in your study of the cornet or trumpet as I have found them in mine.

Earl D. Irons.

Tongue Control

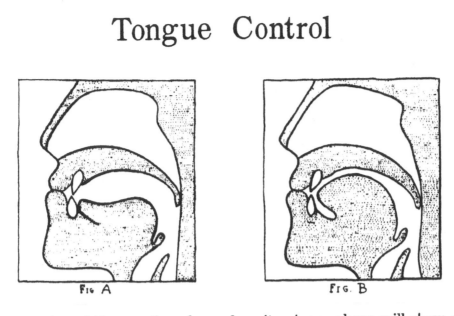

Fig A   Fig. B

The cut of a cross section of the mouth and nasal cavity shown above will show graphically the use of the tongue in pitch variation. Figure A shows the tongue in the low position, or the position for producing the syllable "ah". Figure B shows the tongue in the high position, or the position for producing the syllable "ee". These represent the positions of the tongue for the lowest and highest tones on your instrument. Between them lie a number of positions for the intermediate notes, positions which may be represented partially by the tongue positions for the vowels in "mat, met, mate, mit," etc. In the actual use of the tongue for pitch variation, it is well to note that rise of tongue is more pronounced between tones in the lower register. Just as the tones possible with the same fingering are closer together in the upper register, so too are the tongue positions closer together, making the rise of the tongue hardly perceptible as it approaches the roof of the mouth.

The exercise printed here illustrates the use of the tongue as described in the preceding paragraph. The student should practice it over many times, until he gets the knack of using his tongue in the proper manner. As he practices, he should concentrate on the position of his tongue as each tone is produced. He should feel the rising and falling of the middle of his tongue as the pitch varies.

The lips should work in unison with the tongue. For the extreme low tones, the lower lip is turned over slightly, away from the upper lip, into the cup of the mouthpiece. As higher tones are played, the lower lip works slightly up toward the upper, as the tongue rises.

The placing of the mouthpiece to the lips is, of course, of great importance and should be governed entirely by the formation of the individual's mouth and teeth. No change in the position of the mouthpiece on the lips should be made without consulting an authority, for the student's habitual position may be entirely correct. To find the most natural position, which is by all means the best, the student should imagine that he is posing for a dignified picture, then place the mouthpiece firmly against his lips without shifting or straining his facial muscles. To avoid strain, the student should play very softly for the first few days, and unless he is on a job that requires loud blowing he should always play softly at least three-fourths of his practice time.

AUTHOR'S NOTE: The student must use the fingering exactly as marked in all exercises to get the full benefit from them. Some of the scales and chords are not exactly true, and the signatures are in some instances purposely marked incorrectly, so that many of the so-called false tones are produced by means of secondary fingering in order to keep the pattern uniform.

Groups 1, 2, 3, and 4.

Almost all fine cornet and trumpet players stress the importance of deep breathing and breath control. All performers on these instruments are aware of this prime principle of cornet playing but most of them treat it too lightly. It is suggested here that the student review the treatment of breathing in any of the numerous fine cornet methods before continuing with his practice. The exercises on the following page are aimed to test the breathing habits of the student. All exercises should be played at first without repeating until the lips are flexible and the breath well under control. The student should not go beyond page five until he can play these exercises as written in one breath at a very slow tempo. When this alone is accomplished, the student should feel that he has already made great progress on the way to fine cornet playing.

Care should be taken that the mouthpiece rests firmly against the lips for the low tones. To play the extreme low tones, it will be necessary to turn the part of the lower lip in the mouthpiece over slightly and away from the upper lip. If this procedure seems difficult, the student may try protruding the lower jaw slightly. This cannot be accomplished in one day, but the student will be able to do the trick in due time.

For the high tones it will be necessary to pull the lower lip slightly in towards the upper lip. This procedure will necessitate the application of a little more power. The movement of the lower lip is all done inside the mouthpiece; there is no shifting. The corners of the mouth are always kept firmly against the teeth, not pulled back intentionally. The tongue is raised and lowered with the tones as explained on page 3. The student should keep these principles in mind and practice all of the exercises on the following page until he can play them easily and clearly, finishing with a full tone on the last note of each exercise, which is an octave below the beginning tone. These low tones at the end of each excercise will teach the turn over of the lower lip.

Too much stress cannot be laid on the importance of the sustained tone exercises in group 3. If played properly at a slow tempo with a steady *crescendo* to *forte* and an equally steady *diminuendo*, this group of exercises will prove a valuable warm-up device and a great aid to intonation.

GROUP 1

GROUP 2

GROUP 3

GROUP 4

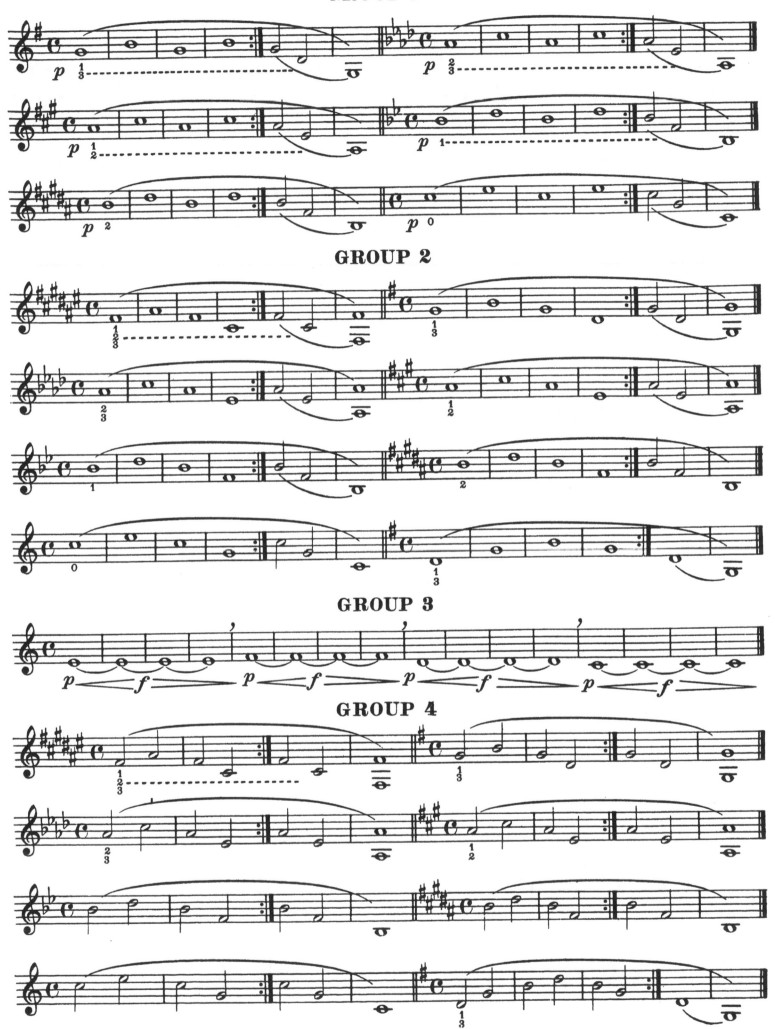

Groups 5, 6, and 7

It is recommended that the exercises in group 5 be played in common time at first. Later, when the tones come easily and clearly without force or strain, the exercises may be played in *alla breve* time and repeated as many times as the student can repeat them and still finish with a clear firm tone on the last note. The last note in each group or phrase is an octave below the starting tone and provides the relaxation of the tongue and lips which is of vital importance to progress in this method of embouchure development.

Group 6 should be played as written, at a moderately slow tempo, and the last tone should be held until the supply of air in the lungs is entirely exhausted.

The seventh group is to be played exactly as written. Attention should be given to the movement of the tongue while these exercises are being played. Although the lips and the facial muscles are important factors in the performance of these exercises, the student should feel that he is varying the pitch of his instrument by raising and lowering his tongue as explained by the illustrations on page 3 of this book.

GROUP 5

GROUP 6

GROUP 7

Groups 8, 9, and 10

Group 8 is but a continuation of the material in Group 7, with an increase in the range of the notes. Each exercise should be repeated four to six times before the last measure is played. The student must always remember that the final tone of each group is important; if these tones do not come easily and clearly, the student is either fatigued or needs further practice on the preceding exercises. Sometimes intensive practice of sustained tones on the low notes, played very softly, is necessary for the proper relaxation of muscles and the correct turn-over of the lower lip inside the mouthpiece.

Groups 6, 7, and 8 are key exercises to the type of embouchure development advocated here. The author personally practices these three exercises more frequently than any others in the book.

Group 9 is to be started slowly, and the speed gradually increased until a reasonably fast tempo is reached.

There are two styles of phrasing, both of equal importance, in Group 10. The author suggests slurring all notes at first and observing the articulation marks later. Group 10 should not be played too fast. The last tone of each group is to be played with a strong accent.

GROUP 8

GROUP 9

GROUP 10

Groups 11, 12, and 13

By this time the student should have realized the importance of fully inflating the lungs before beginning each phrase. Each exercise in Groups 11 and 12 should be repeated many times in one breath. Especial attention is called to the *ritardando* at the end of each exercise in Group 11. During the *ritardando* the student will be conscious of the relaxation and lowering of the tongue, and the turning over of the lower lip inside the mouthpiece for the extreme low tones.

Group 13 is a very interesting one, if played at first with three counts to the measure and the tempo gradually increased until there is only one count to the measure. Strict observance of the accent on the first note of the second measure in each group will insure perfect rhythm. The last phrase may be played very rapidly with a slight exaggeration of accent on the first note of each measure. This exercise will also be found interesting and helpful when single-tongued rather than slurred, with fingering as marked.

GROUP 11

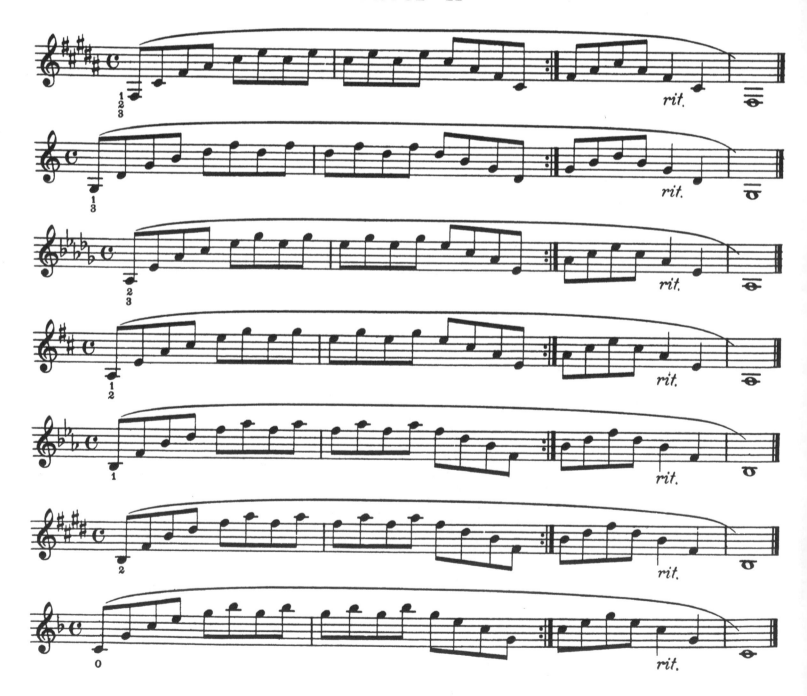

GROUP 12

GROUP 13

Groups 14, 15, and 16

Group 14 is based on the alternate raising and lowering of the middle of the tongue. Each count contains three notes of rising or lowering pitch, with a strong accent on the first of each count. The student will feel the rising and falling of the tongue directly with the pitch. Now that the student has become conscious of this principle of pitch variation he should apply it to his everyday practice of all types of exercises.

Lest the student tend to overlook the importance of sustained tones, the next two groups are introduced for further strengthening the embouchure in all registers. Group 15, if played each morning before breakfast, will be of inestimable benefit both to the elementary student and to the advanced player. It is not recommended that the sustained tones higher than G above the staff, in Group 16, be practiced before the student has acquired a better than average embouchure. By adding a tone at a time as the embouchure develops, the player will find that he can play the notes above the staff with the same ease and clarity as those in the staff.

GROUP 14

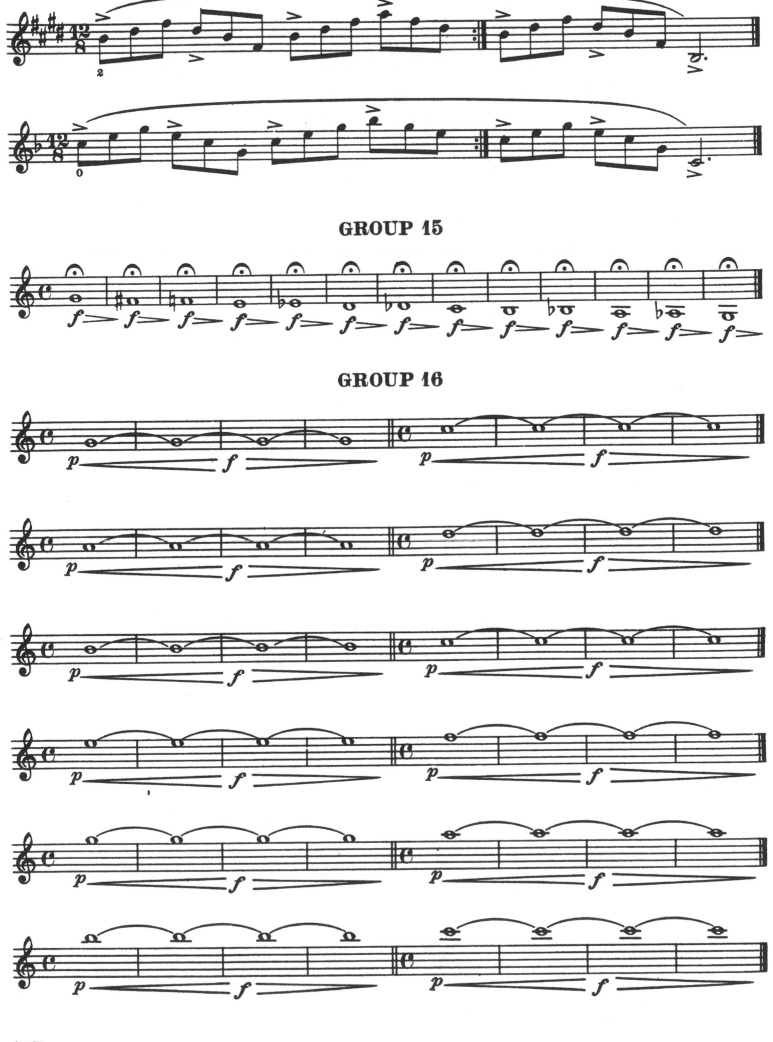

GROUP 15

GROUP 16

Groups 17, 18, and 19

Groups 17, 18, and 19 are excellent exercises for intonation as well as for muscular development. The fingering, as marked, is not, of course, the true fingering in every case. However, the false tones, or tones in which the fingering is a secondary fingering, can be played in tune if proper care is given to the use of the lips. These groups are to be played slowly, both tongued and slurred, with the fingering as marked and repeated many times until all of the tones are played perfectly in tune. When this is accomplished, and the student feels confident of his ability to play all of the notes in tune with the given fingering, he may increase his speed gradually, always listening to his intonation. While speed is not the important thing in these groups, it is well to play them as rapidly as possible with complete clarity and absence of strain.

GROUP 17

GROUP 18

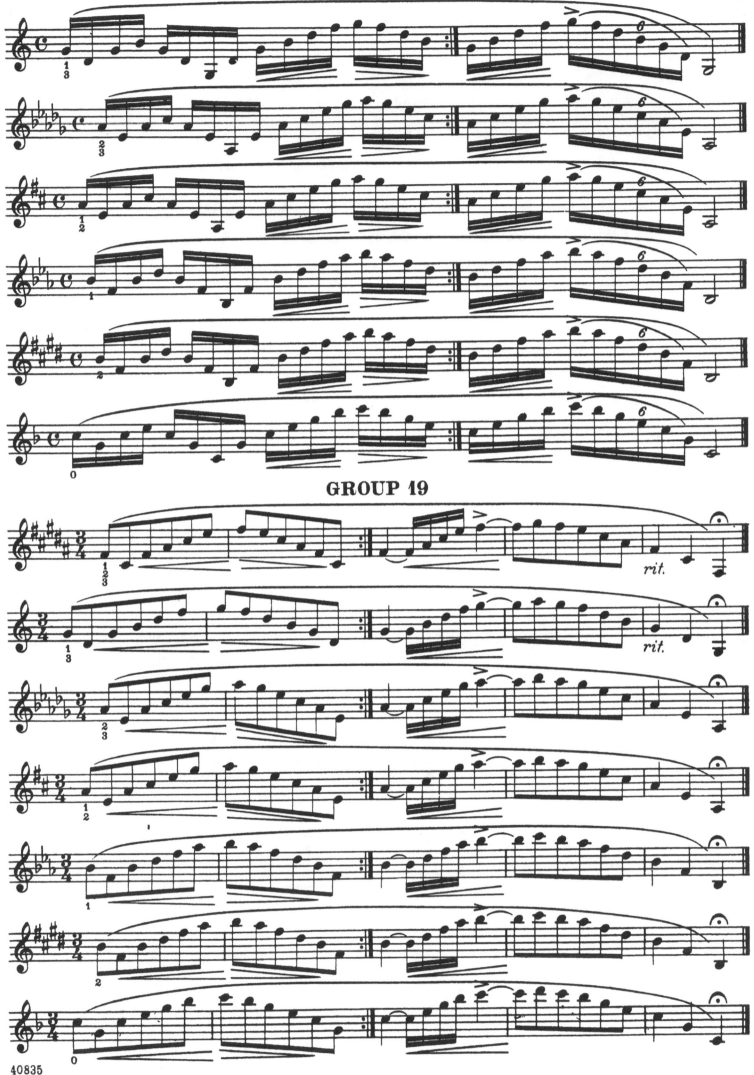

GROUP 19

Groups 20, 21, and 22

Group 20 is a study in intervals, a very necessary type of exercise as is evidenced by the stress placed on interval studies in the many fine methods already generally used. The particular value of this group of exercises lies in strict attention to the *ffz* markings. If the student finds exercise 3 of this group too difficult, he should pass it up and return to it when his embouchure is sufficiently developed.

Groups 21 and 22 contain the most valuable exercises in this book; the range of each exercise covers two octaves and a third. The last exercise in each group should be played with as much ease as the first. The extreme high tones will require more force of breath than the low ones, but should not be accompanied by any strain on the muscles actually involved in the tone production.

Group 21 should first be played slowly with three counts to the measure, and the speed gradually increased until the student is able to play two measures to the count. When this is done, the effect obtained is that of a mallet run rapidly up and down the bars of a xylophone. Group 22 also should be begun at a slow speed and played in common time as written. As the lips become more flexible, the speed is to be increased to two counts to the measure, and then to one count to the measure. When the student is able to play the full sixteen notes in one count, he should repeat each exercise many times before playing the last measure.

GROUP 20

GROUP 21

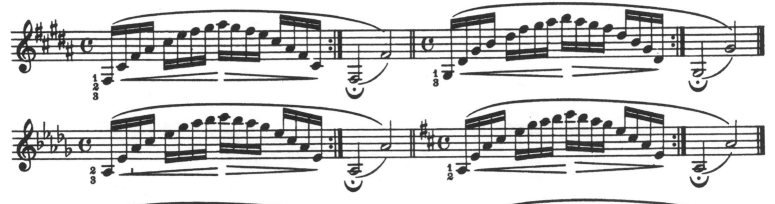

GROUP 22

Groups 23 and 24

Group 23 will require perseverance on the part of the student. Unless the embouchure has already reached a high degree of perfection, the student should limit himself to the first two or three exercises of this group until such a time that the more difficult exercises are possible without undue strain.

Group 24 is an exercise on the tongue trill, commonly called the lip trill. No elaborate approach to the trill will be given in this work, for adequate explanation of the lip trill has been given in many other fine cornet methods. However, a brief discussion of the execution of the trill will be in order. In playing the trill, the tongue is used in much the same manner as in whistling a trill. The tip of the tongue rests lightly at the base of the lower teeth. The middle of the tongue is moved rapidly up and down. To perfect this motion, the student should practice saying the syllables *a-ee, a-ee* very rapidly aloud. This gives the approximate movement of the tongue during the trill. If the student practices diligently he will not find it difficult to play the trill on notes above F#, top line. He should begin by practicing the trill on F#, top line, G, and G#,[1] and working on the trill for several days before attempting the exercises in Group 24, for the exercises are really impossible unless the trill can be properly executed.

It is well worth the student's time to perfect the lip trill. The trill is not a mere trick of showmanship, but can be made an integral part of solo playing which will be especially effective and brilliant in cadenzas.

[1] The student should finger the notes as follows while practicing the trill: F# 123, G 13, G# 123.

GROUP 23

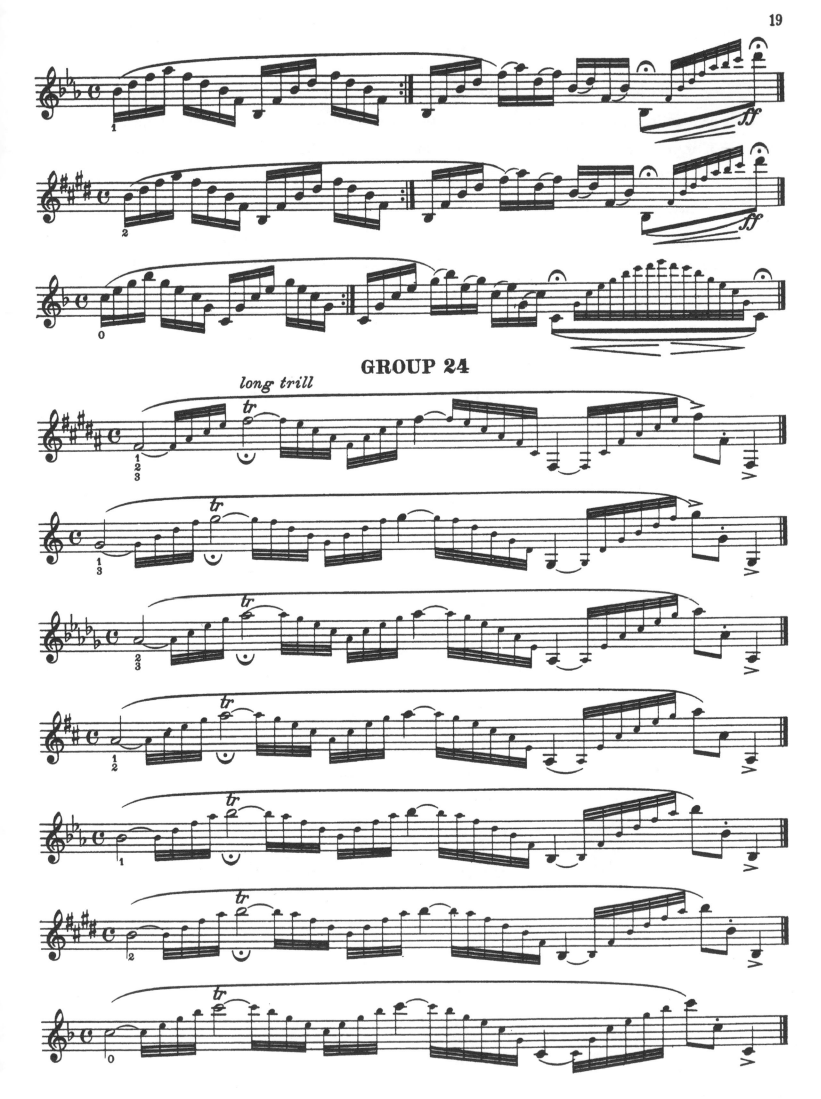

GROUP 24

long trill

Groups 25 and 26

It is hoped that judgment will be exercised in playing the extreme high tones of Group 25. These tones should not be practiced too soon nor too often. If the student cannot play F and G above high C—without undue strain or pressure it is better not to attempt those tones at all. In fact, this group of exercises is by way of being a test of the embouchure development. If the student has devoted sufficient time and diligent effort to the preceding exercises in this book, he will encounter no serious difficulty in playing Groups 25 and 26 as written. The author of this work plays them about twice every day, but it must be remembered that he has spent many months practicing all of the exercises in this book, and still seldom lets a day pass without playing through the entire collection.

Group 25 finishes the portion of this book devoted to embouchure development alone. Group 26 offers the student an opportunity to use the strengthened embouchure in tongued and fingered exercises. In Group 26, the measures from A to B can be omitted, and should be omitted unless the embouchure is sufficiently developed to permit their execution without undue strain. If the student pinches or squeezes the high tones and cannot play them clearly at a stinging *forte,* he is merely deceiving himself as to his ability to play high tones. He should review some of the preceding exercises, especially Groups 6, 7, 8, 21, and 22.

GROUP 25

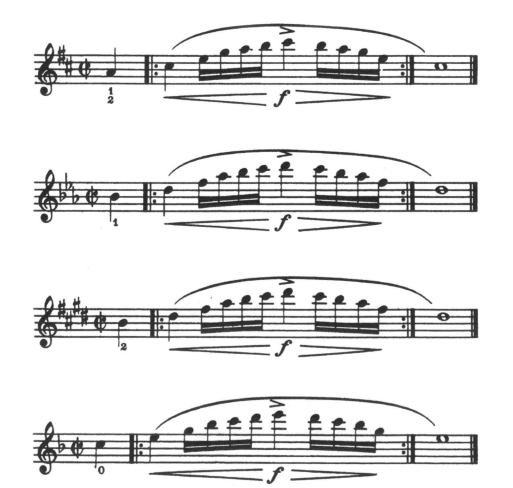

GROUP 26

Group 27

The chromatic exercises in Group 27 are written with key signatures in order to make them more interesting and more valuable from the standpoint of reading. Each exercise is short; the first one can be practiced as soon as the student is able to play C above the staff, and succeeding exercises can be added as the embouchure is developed to take care of the higher tones. These exercises can be played in three counts or in one, at the will of the student, but never so fast that any note is slighted.

After the student has played through all of the exercises in this group, he should not feel that he has finished with the book. He should keep it as a handbook for embouchure maintenance. To hold what he has gained, he must play through the entire book often. Furthermore, he will find that playing the first exercise in each group offers a very effective warm-up device. The author often has his advanced students begin their lessons with this device.

GROUP 27

PART II
Triple and Double Tonguing Exercises

Play the F scale up one octave using the above pattern.

Play exercise No. 30 starting very slow. Repeat each two measures many times increasing spead each time.

28

29

30

31

32

30

40835

45

45a

45b

45c

45d

46